Prison Segmentation For Spiral Path Circuit Connections

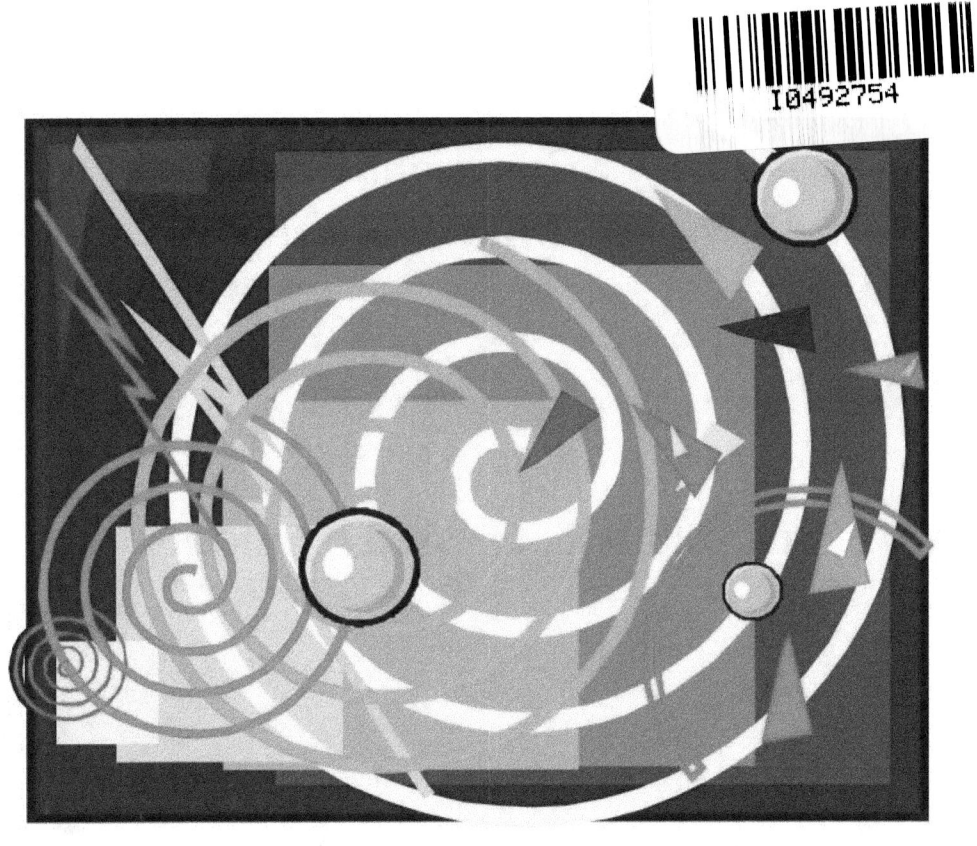

Freedom Spirals

Rev. Mike Wanner

Table of Contents

Introduction

I have been writing a lot about prisons and realized that the complexity is rooted in a constant of change which means that reassessment is increasingly necessary to attain a viewpoint that is timely. Unfortunately, change has been slow, and that can complicate everything.

Multiple path circuits can help perspective possibilities and provide access options for staff that can help ensure minimum interacting with prisoners for maximum safety and security. A bit of protection can save taxpayers a lot of money.

Safety is important because injuries to prison staff and prisoners can be costly and disruptive. Security, of course, is priceless.

1 - Why I am Writing This Book

I have been absolutely amazed at the complexity of the whole prison situation and the variety of rules and authorities that oversee the various facilities.

I want to offer some ideas here for consideration. My views may not be practical in every facility because of design differences, regulating authorities and geographical variables.

I intend to fully root this book and all my others in the idea that each individual desires and deserves dignity. Respect for many people is not given because the one who could offer it may lack the understanding of what it is and how one shows it to other people.

All too often recently, you hear people demand respect, and within that demand, they lack respect for the one who they wish to show it to them. You can explain it and grow it but not receive it from ones who do not have or understand it.

You may not have appreciated respect when you were growing up. When I read about the prisons and the courts and the treatment of prisoners, I am always aware of the impersonal nature of the process.

In my experience, a little consideration goes a long way. I invite readers to self-test themselves for sensitivity to others.

A good reason to be respectful is that it is the right thing to do. Another excellent reason to do it is that it can be a much less stressful and much more productive way to live.

2 - The Love Fear Continuum

Angel Raphael Speaks Message set 9 there is a message titled *Prison Life of the Future*, and from that, I quote the last paragraphs below.

"…Please consider as if the vibration of a prison existed on a scale that you could read called the love fear continuum. Consider that a single increment move on that scale that went away from fear and moved towards love was actually beneficial to all who passed through the premises.

As you ever so slightly held that thought, you entertained the possibility of a shift for the imprisoned and guards of the future. Congratulations, for you, have allowed some light to shine on a subject that is almost perpetually locked in pessimism." ARS 9

Moving away from fear allows a whole spectrum of possibilities for all connected to the one who is being freed. It is entirely possible that the less physical ones who are free from fear may also be the most creative ones who could power up the potential for enhancing the lives of the whole community.

Being free from the fear of the general population could motivate the candidates to work hard to help the system so that they never outlive their utility. Once freed relatively, they could soar conceptually to benefit even those that they might have feared.

3 - The Alzheimer's Circle

After returning home from Vietnam, I went back to Sears Roebuck and Company and got to work. Shortly thereafter, I started volunteering for the Ambulance Organization which helped my father for almost a year before he died.

The volunteer work led to me starting an ambulance Company and working professionally in the field for twenty-five Years. Doing that work brought me in touch with all the adverse experiences that impact so many citizens.

Sickness and drug addiction were the afflictions of those who I sought to help, and I paid attention and learned. I wanted to share here what I thought was the neatest management tool for people in an altered state of mental illusion.

There were a lot of patients who had Alzheimer disease and wanted to walk around the premises. It was difficult for caregivers to manage them and keep them where they were supposed to be so they could be medicated on schedule.

Trying to constrict the patients caused conflict and that could create outbursts and the need for restraints so they would not hurt themselves, other patients, or staff. Breakthrough thinking lead to locked circular units where patients were free to go around and walk to their heart's content because as they went away, they were on the path to return.

No injuries, no conflict, no kicking, no screaming and no hassle whatsoever.

4 - Minimal Confrontation Management

I propose a progressive exploration and expansion of this concept for facilities that have too many conflicts in their operations. The graphic that I used has many variables, and I would like to offer some interpretations to play within that analysis later in this book.

Please note there are

- Wide Spirals

- Big Circles

- Squares

- Little circles

- Triangles

- A short two-line closed curve

- Integration points between many things

- Lightening like jagged sections

- One extension reaches outside the big block.

- Other lines reach close to or adjacent to the outside perimeter

5 - Appropriate Application Target

Solitary Community was a book that I wrote earlier that may be an excellent place to start. Solitary may be the most costly and risky of the sections within many prisons.

The administration could investigate possibilities to use segmentation along with a spiral path and traditionally not accessed space on an expanded access time basis.

One step at a time. Let's ask some questions to stimulate thought.

1. Is there a prisoner in solitary who might be responsive to increased freedom and kindness?

2. What might the prisoner see as a benefit?

3. What steps could be taken without any extra expense that could:

    A. Give the prisoner more space/freedom than s/he ever had before.

    B. Give the prisoner that freedom without any commitment on their part.

    C. Give the prisoner more time freedom than s/he ever had before.

    D. Schedule the initial efforts in a way that no other activities are impacted.

6 - Solitary Segmentation Start

My messages about segmentation were mostly directed to the general population, so I will put some effort here toward mixing segmentation, some access efforts and movements within Solitary in a little bit more depth of detail.

Adding variables to shift patterning may not be feasible in some facilities, but I will put some things down to be considered. I do welcome feedback to my e-mail so please write to reverendmikewanner@aol.com.

None of this will be accomplishable without straightforward creativity from cooperating staff members and residents. I understand that my messages may seem somewhat controversial and the words on these pages do not have all the needed background information to be a successful plan.

I feel that pattern reformation can be a positive step that could help make positive changes. I find no fault with the hierarchy of what has been because people usually do the best they can with what they have in the system that they are working within.

The best that was available years ago when some policies were enacted may be dated and somewhat unworkable. Everything can change and improve over time and perhaps now is a good time to do that.

Moving forward let us regroup and rethink the path ahead. The density of persons in prison could contribute to stress that could be a significant element of the lack of cooperation that might be seen as resistance.

The idea behind segmentation is to work with people who would not mind being up and about in shifting hours when the prison might be otherwise quiet. Moving around in an area while most people are sleeping elsewhere in the building could give the willing participants a feeling of temporary spatial freedom that could be very peaceful.

If you think of a time when you got up in the middle of the night to leave for a long trip, you might experience the feeling of satisfaction when there is no one on the road but you.

Prisoners who are very crowded in sleeping accommodations may be very willing to change from a single shift to a choice of variations that allow more freedom of movement and fewer feelings of congestion and invasion of their personal space.

Destressing the space available to prisoners by spreading people out can allow for less stress and more peace. Doing that in solitary can be a game changer.

Ideas for the first Attempt:

1. Try to give a private invitation to one resident at a time until somebody says yes.

2. Make sure each invitee understands that this is a declinable invitation without any penalty for saying no.

3. Make sure each invitee understands that this could be a one-time event or a repeating event and their suggestions will be invited afterward.

4. They will be among the evaluators of this effort.

5. Staff may find value in identifying positive responders as a titled group with a name chosen to enhance the appeal of participation.

6. Select a time block movement where they will be free to move along a familiar path as they wish with recommendations for their consideration.

7. It may be helpful to give early respondents a choice of time blocks they could move around within. For example, if solitary is usually locked down between 11PM and 7 AM and their total out of cell time usually is one hour: You might consider offering a two-hour movement path in blocks of time like 11PM- 1AM, 2AM-3AM, 3AM - 5AM, and %AM-7AM.

8. They might just be happy to have a bit of free choice and surprise staffers with cooperation.

7 - Voluntary or Required Movement

While the path of movement for a solitary prisoner is very minimal, it seems that the suggestion here is to find constructive, progress and creative ways to move the prisoner along their required path circuit in a schedule that is less challenging to all. In the Alzheimer patient circuit discussed above, the idea was to allow choices to avoid confrontation.

In this concept allowing freedom in a different way is the idea to be discussed. Here we want to talk about using space as a motivator for movement along a circuit that is routine but doing that in a way that allows the prisoners to experience more of the concepts of freedom and choice.

Please understand that this will not be a mass movement of people over a small time but a single movement of one person. In the early stages at least, efforts can be optimal by just seeing what can be done to change the pattern and motivation subtly for a single prisoner and then use the experience gained to increase outcomes and pattern recording.

Free choices can be a powerful motivation, and this whole country was created to be able to have those choices. Not shabby at all that.

Of course, naysayers might pipe up with traditional lines of thought that indicate old thinking and I understand that pattern. The opportunity here is to think differently and create new designs that improve the prisoner experience, and staff safety as the requirements of the court and community are complied with in exacting required specificity.

Creative thinking can provide some flexibility for the most people, and that can lessen risk and the avoidable confrontations. Peaceful interactions can save a lot in the system by avoiding the need for treatment and staff rehabilitation.

The most critical element of this approach may well be the lessening of a need for peacekeeping so there can be a bit more time available for some positivity and maybe even some rehabilitation. Would that not be wonderful?

Solitary shifts can prove monumentally helpful in the further design of program upgrades by setting an example of accomplishments possible. If something works in solitary with the least cooperative prisoners possible, would it not be applicable also in general populations.

No Cost Criteria

We need to eliminate the excuse of money. We need no-cost solutions that make common sense clear and fiscal responsibility evident.

Not only do our solutions need not cost anything, but they also need to save pain, suffering, and annoyance to staff and administration. In outside world terms, we need no-brainers.

Mental moods can impact these criteria so the thinkers are encouraged to do the thinking at the most appropriate times. We can do reality checks and raise the bar projections.

8 - Staff Concept Completers Needed

What you think matters as it forms the foundation for all that you will consider or reject. Please ask yourself some questions:

1. How can we implement this idea in Solitary?

2. What would the effect be in your institution?

3. Who can be helped first with this idea?

4. What can you do to develop the idea?

5. What are all the risks now?

6. What is your exposure to those who participate?

7. How Could this idea benefit staff?

8. How Could this idea benefit prisoners?

9. If you won't participate, what freedom would you lose?

9 - Circuit Motivators

Starting in solitary can offer some safety when staff can trigger the wanting of the solitary occupants to move where the team would like them to be at their own free will.

Motivators could include:

- Music Stations with headphones
- TV access
- Meal flexibility
- Yard Access
- Timed snack access
- Timed Coffee break access
- Communication with others via:
  - Phone
  - Adjacent meeting spots with talk between possible
  - Movie discussions possibilities
  - Limited Twitter access
  - Limited E-mail access

10 - Steady Expectation Conditioning

The plan is to move forward progressively and create expectations that are most aligned with staff safety and prisoner peace. Prison is stressful already, and those who have been assigned to solitary may be even more highly stressed.

To the degree that we can change and manage expectations, we will be initiating subtle influence on the will of the prisoners to cooperate instead of fighting everything.

Replacing the boredom of solitary with the freedom of segmentation can go a long way to start a willingness of the prisoner to cooperate with the motivation of a segmented solitary. Each effort can incrementally expand the parameters of the conditioning and progressively create an incentive for expanded effort.

Additionally, the subtle shift in each effort will stifle the boredom of the regular mediocrity. The point may be reached where the variation could take on a healing dynamic of its own.

Ironic maybe the assembly of variations to a much more healing reality than the standard protocol dynamics. In this situation, they actually change behavior and then demonstrate the ability to adapt to changing circumstances.

.

11 - The Expansion of Choice

Solitary confinement is suggested as a starting point because success there could have many side effects that are beneficial. Another reason would be that efforts could be specifically targeted to be strategically observed so the lessons can be reviewed and expanded.

The smallest increment of variation would be a place to start. You could look at the path that one prisoner takes every day anyhow and see what could be activated to facilitate that without any additional exposure for staff.

Little baby steps start with just enough additional freedom to be noticed while maintaining absolutely all standard safety, security and protocol rules.

It is frequently reported that many people in solitary only get about an hour outside their space. Consider the experience of the prisoner who doubles that or triples that or quadruples that and whether that might just be a great day for that individual.

Would one great day have an influence on their future flexibility standards and their willingness to cooperate even slightly better than their correction officers have been accustomed to expect? Based on the results experienced by the prisoners and the observations of staff, repetition of the effort could be initiated to see just how must progress one prisoner could make in one application.

Steady evaluation is suggested, and documentation would be pivotal to the success of this idea in other areas.

12 - Expanding the Freedom Further

Depending on the location and the distances and the normal flow of prisoners, it would be great if there could be a progressive goal series of steps set to double the total freedom of choice options. I wrote an earlier book about access controls which could be considered in itty bitty steps to allow movement in a progressive way.

Cost containment can be a significant accelerator so planning will be pivotal. Access controls can be little switch circuits or computerized systems depending upon the complexity.

Adding segmentation concepts could allow expansion of staff creativity and security. Staff focus on optimal results might be helped by anticipating the thought patterns of the prisoners that will enable as much as possible, more choices to move as motivated by their internal inclinations toward acceptance and participation.

Collaboration with others builds potential for success after re-entry to the world that focuses on independence in an acceptable interactive way through courtesy and respect. These skills could be priceless gifts that help re-entered prisoners peacefully adjust to any future conflicting opinions.

The mental muscle of versatility can equip participants well for the type of teamwork they will need when they return to the free society outside the wall and all the variations of the kinds of people who they will find there.

13 - Delay Announcement of The Effort

It may not make a lot of sense to start announcing the effort because it could take a while for anybody to understand the possibilities of this idea. If you are able to cut come costs that are measurable with some trial efforts of this concept, Administration may get some reward funding as a ramp up to additional savings possibilities.

Accurate reporting of cost-benefit will be needed, or the efficiency triggers may not get recognized.

Expanding the Circuit

As reports come in that save a little bit, Documentation would be valuable as progress could be determined by the quality of the paperwork. Prisons have huge expenses so money may need to follow the greatest need for the highest number of people.

Well documented successes could well make the difference in how far the idea spreads and how many people are helped. For me, the most significant goal would be the safety of staff members by constructively avoiding adverse interactions and allowing freedom of movement to incentivize the prisoners to move about freely on a more active basis.

If your prison starts the idea in solitary, your ingenuity will be essential but also will be a plan B if there are episodes of pushback. Please try to convey in the perfectly right way, that cooperation equals freedom and resistance reverses freedom.

14 - Participation Candidates

For this concept to have a possibility for success, selection of candidates would need to be diligent. Who might be most motivated to embrace the reward and wish to see it continue?

If your prison introduces this idea in a segment that is split off of the general population, it could be easier to find those who are most at risk. They could be very compliant to a circuit that increased their safety from others who might be unfriendly to them for any reason.

When people who are in fear for any reason can find a bit of safety, their appreciation can be extremely helpful to those in authority.

Some residents of prisons might stand out as candidates for rehabilitation who could do it themselves if they had a little bit of peace and order in their living and working space.

Frequently victimized residents may become very helpful if there is enough space security for them to focus on their gifts and offer up support efforts which contribute to the community peace and harmonious efforts for the greater good.

We could easily see that secure segments could be used differently than order and control situations. Prisoners and staff relations could have significant improvement when there are recognizable planning and order alignments separate from the influences of any disruptive groups within the whole place.

15 - What's Possible

I sincerely believe that Solitary more than any other segment will be fruitful or shelved based on the level of engagement and creativity of the correctional officers that have the crucial information. It could go well if officers are able to think outside the patterns that they have been conditioned with as they have been brought up through the system.

Line and staff organizations members understand that they need to follow the rules or at least be somewhat close to the guidelines. To do that in this project may be too tedious for the average staff member.

The successful corrections staffer will be the one who can dip into the details and make a case for protocol expansion based on recorded results. This will not be precisely easy but could explode the career of the detailed developer in an expansive way which might be great for their job or a mere memorandum of willingness to work towards a goal.

If I were the one in that position, I would endeavor to be creative and yet careful to detail sufficiently that the options delivered was phrased for a decision maker who had sufficient security to stick out their neck and make calls that were experimental yet based on thorough documentation.

16 - Flow

A little planning could move the vulnerable residents from danger and set them up to help and be recognized for their ideas and contributions to spreading order and psychological peace. Let's project from the cover image photo and then conceptualize plans for the use of space within the big picture.

The image used on the cover here is very different from the straight lines that are quite universal in prisons. The addition of the various shapes and sizes add variation to the theme of a big box, and that is like so indicative I believe of the kinds of things that we might consider for prisons going forward.

While the shapes may trigger different ideas in a group assembled to discuss them, there can also be the definition of space as agreement comes to those gathered of how space can be efficiently utilized. As one participant makes a recommendation for a particular shape, the ideas for all can be voted and agreed, discussed, modified and set as determined.

Let's have a discussion about the shapes within the picture and all the potentials where the forms intercept where an access system could provide a variety of optional paths.

The shapes are not indicative of a new pattern for all prisons but merely an idea that the old models may be limiting concepts and flows and security options. Each prison will be different, and the administration is invited to play with the shapes and sizes and also develop their own.

Of course, security reviews of all possibilities would be needed to ensure it does not work against the administration. The shapes are:

- Wide Spirals and tight spirals - May be helpful in creating pathways that increase security.

- Big Circles - Could be meeting spaces for teams of perspective.

- Squares – May represent some traditional components of the system.

- Little circles – Could be individual respite spots for cooperative residents with further access.

- Triangles -Could be Library or function spaces for :
    1) Twitter
    2) Community E-mail with scrutiny
    3) Message to Kids console
    4) Message to Spouse console
    5) Music breaks

- Short two-line closed curve – Secondary Circuits

- Integration points between many things – Places where access controls can eventually change the flow dynamics.

- Lightening like jagged sections – Express Paths

- One extension reaches outside the big block - More options.

- Other lines reach close to or adjacent to the outside perimeter – More Options

17 - More Access for Cooperative Residents

Prisoners who are cooperative may the perfect candidates to get expanded access either with keycards or controlled access systems. Access and segmentation can make the options under all circumstance much more optimal than the general mass movement of people.

The freedom of access will mean different things to different people, so it is essential to be aware of what the residents are thinking. Segmentation can help a lot with that so please consider using what is available.

The more that impersonal treatment of residents is minimized, the more likely will be the expansion of cooperation and a peaceful prison.

Prison today may be excellent in control, but not too good at hospitality. Alpha male dynamics are not real cooperative elements of a peaceful interactive community.

We all can learn that civility can carry us to opportunities that would not exist without it. More Freedom carries the joys of a life well, and more freedom can bring more happiness.

Joy is a great goal, and as we move from where we are to where we want to be. We can decide to endure well the awkwardness of running against our ingrained experience.

Key cards to increase access within appropriate parameters and timelines can extend cooperative demeanors and shift the patterns of interaction between prisoners and staff as well as between prisoner and other prisoners.

As cooperation increases so do the potential for optimal safety as well as the opportunity for appropriately expressing what is needed to maintain and or increase the teamwork.

18 - Circuit Benefits

There is an old benefit in planning design that can improve the quality of life for those moving through places. The design system that can help with this is called Feng Shui, and it works well in many spaces.

Prisons are not likely to have a system in place that is organized around the flow of energy and the impacts that space can have on the people who move through the rooms. No system tweaks deliver no benefit tweaks, and the way things are is a clearly understood institutional reality.

Prisons are organized in a way that focuses on controlling the space and in that pursuit human sensitivity is less than prominent. The effect on humans is like a dam on a river in that the flow is constricted and pressure is concentrated.

Spiral Path Circuits can offer reasonable efforts to reduce pressure and allow flow that is kind and gentle to the residents and staff in a way that diminishes oppressive control and increases safety options, freedoms, and more relaxed space.

19 - Wrap Up

Reasonable efforts to provide pattern changes which increase human kindness would be challenging to criticise if diligence in safety for the staff was raised in the process. Crises for the prisoner receiving the consideration could be stabilized.

There is much here that can be easily quantified and precisely evaluated from a cost standpoint. Even if efforts merely prevented cost escalation and prisoner confrontations, the initiative would have great value in destressing the facility, providing more options for staff and allowing peaceful sentence serving opportunities.

A better work environment for staffers and perhaps a foundation place for rehabilitation can bloom for prisoners, the prison staff, and all their families.

Blessed Be All Who Read These Words, AND SO IT IS!

For
Considering
These
Ideas

Ever

It Does Not Help Prayer Still Does!

Resource: http://Create-A-Prayer.com

22 - Book Resources
at www.Amazon.com

Distant Healing (or Mail List) e-mail mikewann@voicenet.com

Veterans Healing Six Pack Books plus 2
http://angelraphaelspeaks.com/healing-books/veterans/

PTSD Power Pack Books
http://angelraphaelspeaks.com/healing-books/ptsd/

Angel Raphael Speaks Series & Other Angel Books
http://angelraphaelspeaks.com/

Reiki Books
http://angelraphaelspeaks.com/healing-books/reiki/

Children's Books
http://angelraphaelspeaks.com/healing-books/children/

Emergency Medical Kindness Books
http://angelraphaelspeaks.com/healing-books/emergency-medical-kindness/

Cancer Books
http://angelraphaelspeaks.com/healing-books/cancer/

Addictions Books
http://angelraphaelspeaks.com/healing-books/addictions/

Healing Books
http://angelraphaelspeaks.com/healing-books/misc-healing/

Prison Books - 50+ Prison Books
http://angelraphaelspeaks.com/prison-books/

23 - Angels Please Prayers

Addict's

Angels of Healing Selected
Help Me to Stay Directed
Come To Me From The Sky
I Am Ready to Succeed Not Try
If I Don't Invite You In
I Might Not Win
I Have Been Lost For Too Long
Help Me To Stay Strong

&

Alcoholic's

Angels of Healing On High
Help Me to Stay Dry
Come To Me From The Sky
I Am Ready to Succeed Not Try
If I Don't Invite You In
I Might Not Win
I Have Been Lost For Too Long
Help Me To Stay Strong

From

http://AngelRaphaelSpeaks.com/AAAAAAA/

24 - Private Channeling

Angel Raphael Speaks a series of free messages that are channeled through Reverend Mike Wanner for the Highest good and Highest Healing of all concerned.

Many questions arise about Reverend Mike doing private channeling, and he does help with that so E-mail him.

Reverend Mike is available worldwide as a psychic channel, emotional release facilitator, spiritual energy practitioner & teacher, and public speaker. He looks forward to meeting you soon!

Email - mikewann@voicenet.com 215-342-1270

PRIVATE SPIRITUAL READINGS/channelings or Spiritual Healing Sessions: Telephone or in person.

Rev. Mike is available for individual, intuitive one-on-one sessions with you, his Guide Family, and your Guides. He helps by offering clarity on emotional situations about your life, your purpose, your spirituality, and your release of stuffed emotions and cellular memory.

Connect to the love of your Guides today!

For more information, Please visit
http://angelraphaelspeaks.com/channel/

25 - Reverend Mike Wanner

Rev. Mike Wanner started his spiritual and ministerial studies with Reiki in 1993 and had studied seven styles of Reiki in the U.S., Japan, Canada, Denmark and Australia. He is certified to teach. He became certified to teach Integrated Energy Therapy in 1999 and co-taught the first IET class of the new Millennium. Mike began dowsing in 2001.

Ordained as an Interfaith Minister of the Circle of Miracles Ministry and a Metaphysical Minister of the International Metaphysical Ministry, Rev. Mike practices and teaches spiritual energy therapies in the Philadelphia Area.

Rev. Mike holds ministerial degrees from the University of Metaphysics and the University of Sedona. He is a Pastoral Care Associate at Jefferson - Frankford Hospital. He taught at the National Academy of Massage Therapy and Health Sciences.

Rev. Mike was a faculty member of the Medical Mission Sister's Center for Human Integration's School of Integrated Body/Mind Therapies in Fox Chase, Philadelphia, PA for twelve years.

For a complete Biography, Please visit
http://ReverendMikeWanner.com/Bio

www.ingramcontent.com/pod-product-compliance
Lightning Source LLC
Chambersburg PA
CBHW071201220526
45468CB00003B/1114

* 9 7 8 1 7 2 2 1 3 3 7 4 0 *